HISTORY & CHRISTIANITY
JOHN WARWICK MONTGOMERY

InterVarsity Press
Downers Grove, Illinois 60515

Fifth printing, September 1976
©1964 and 1965 by Inter-Varsity
Christian Fellowship of the United
States of America. All rights
reserved. No part of this book may be
reproduced in any form without written
permission from InterVarsity Press.

InterVarsity Press is the book
publishing division of Inter-Varsity
Christian Fellowship, a student
movement active on campus at
hundreds of universities, colleges
and schools of nursing. For information
about Inter-Varsity Christian
Fellowship, write IVCF,
233 Langdon St., Madison, WI 53703.

The Scripture quotations in this
publication are from the Revised
Standard Version of the Bible, copy-
righted 1946 and 1952 by the Division
of Christian Education of the National
Council of the Churches of Christ in the
U.S.A., and used by permission.

First published December 1964 through
March 1965 in HIS, the monthly
student magazine of Inter-Varsity
Christian Fellowship. To subscribe,
write HIS, 5206 Main, Downers
Grove, Illinois 60515.

ISBN 0-87784-437-2
Library of Congress Catalog
Card Number: 78-160367

Printed in the United States
of America

CONTENTS

FOREWORD

The present book has an interesting history. Its origin dates to January 1963 when Professor John Warwick Montgomery delivered two lectures called "Jesus Christ and History" at the University of British Columbia. Mimeograph copies circulated in Canada for some time. Then these lectures became a series of four articles published by HIS magazine, December 1964 to March 1965. Subsequently the articles were issued and widely distributed as a HIS reprint.

Inter-Varsity Press is now pleased to issue these articles in more permanent form.

Added as an appendix is "Faith, History and the Resurrection"—a vigorous panel discussion involving Dr. Montgomery, Dr. William Hordern, Dr. Jules L. Moreau, Father Sergius Wroblewski, Dr. Kenneth Kantzer and Dr. Carl F. H. Henry. This discussion with panelists who represent several divergent positions directly relates to the material in Dr.

Montgomery's articles. The text is the edited transcription of the discussion originally published in *Christianity Today,* March 26, 1965.

There is an interesting aftermath to Dr. Montgomery's original lectures. Since Dr. Montgomery was already corresponding with C. S. Lewis, the Lutheran Student Movement asked him to invite Lewis to lecture at the University of British Columbia, further developing the apologetic issues that had been raised. The following reply was one of the last letters Lewis wrote before his death less than three months later (November 22, 1963). This letter has not appeared in any collection of Lewis's correspondence.

Oxford
29 August 63

Dear Mr. Montgomery,

I am afraid the days of my lecturing and traveling are over. Last July my death was hourly expected, and tho' I didn't get through the gate I have had to resign all my posts and settle down (not unhappily) to the life of an invalid.

Your two lectures did me good and I shall constantly find them useful. Congratulations. The only criticism I'd venture is that you have possibly a little bit over-called the blow about *kyrios.* Admittedly, like Lat. *dominus* and English *Lord,* it may represent JHVH: but like them it can also mean a human superior. The vocative *kyrie* often needs to be translated "Sir" rather than "Lord." Otherwise I don't think it could be bettered.

> *Yours sincerely,*
> C. S. Lewis

The Publisher

1

FOUR COMMON ERRORS

In a philosophy club lecture delivered at the University of British Columbia some time ago Professor Avrum Stroll alleged, according to a Canadian Press dispatch widely publicized, that "a Jesus probably did exist but so many legends have grown about him that it is impossible for scholars to find out anything about the real man," that "the Gospels of St. Matthew, St. Mark, St. Luke and St. John were written long after Jesus was crucified and provide no reliable historical information about him," and that "it is almost impossible to derive historical facts from the legends and descriptions of miracles performed by Jesus." The importance of the questions raised by Professor Stroll and by others today cannot be exaggerated. The following discussion is designed to aid university students to think through these issues for themselves.

Who Is Jesus Christ?

The earliest records we have of the life and ministry of Jesus give the overwhelming impression that this man went around not so much "doing good" but making a decided nuisance of himself.

The parallel with Socrates in this regard is strong: Both men infuriated their contemporaries to such an extent that they were eventually put to death. But where Socrates played the gadfly on the collective Athenian rump by demanding that his hearers "know themselves"—examine their unexamined lives—Jesus alienated his contemporaries by continually forcing them to think through their attitude to him personally. "Who do men say that I the Son of man am? . . . Who do you say that I am?" "What do you think of Christ? whose son is he?" These were the questions Jesus asked.

And it seems patently clear that the questioner was not asking because he really didn't know who Jesus was and needed help in finding out. Unlike the "sick" characters in Jules Feiffer's Greenwich Village cartoons, when Jesus asked, "Who am I?" he was evidently fully aware of his own character; what he sought to achieve by his questions was a similar awareness of his nature by others.

In this book I shall again pose Jesus' irritating questions concerning himself: Who was he? Who did he claim to be? Is there compelling evidence in support of these claims? This chapter and the following one will discuss the documentary basis of Jesus' life and claims, and thereby provide the necessary background for the next two chapters on the divinity of Jesus Christ, in which the claims themselves will be explicitly set forth, together with the attestation for them by way of the resurrection.

In spite of the tension which these issues will engender (they have always done so, since they inevitably require a rethinking of one's personal *Weltanschauung*—one's philosophy of life), I raise the questions with pleasure, since once upon a time, when I was an undergraduate philosophy student at Cornell University, I myself encountered this crucial problem-area, and as a result became a Christian believer. Like Cambridge professor C. S. Lewis, I was brought "kicking and struggling" into the kingdom of God by the historical evidence in behalf of Jesus' claims. The resulting experiential (existential, if you will) satisfaction with the Christian world-view makes me more than willing to present the case for your consideration.

To get at the essential issue, I wish to recount a situation that developed at the University of British Columbia a couple of years ago. Dr. Avrum Stroll of the Philosophy Department delivered a lecture titled, "Did Jesus Really Exist?" Professor Stroll's remarks were widely publicized, and I replied to them in the public press. His position—which I regard as historically untenable—is summed up in the closing sentence of his address: *"An accretion of legends grew up about this figure [Jesus], was incorporated into the gospels by various devotees of the movement, was rapidly spread throughout the Mediterranean world by the ministry of St. Paul; and that [sic] because this is so, it is impossible to separate these legendary elements in the purported descriptions of Jesus from those which in fact were true of him."*[1]

In my judgment, Professor Stroll arrives at this conclusion as a result of committing four serious historical-philosophical errors, and we shall take these up.

But first I wish to indicate that in one very important respect at least, Dr. Stroll and I are in full agreement. President Briggs of the University Philosophy Club declared in a Canadian Press news dispatch following the Stroll lecture, "As a matter of fact we consider these topics, atheism and Jesus Christ, as not very important"—as compared, for example,

---

[1] Stroll's address (with his own corrections) appears as Appendix A of my *Where Is History Going?* (Grand Rapids: Zondervan, 1969), pp. 207-21.

with the question of "whether the earth's ʀ
is running out." On the contrary, I regard th
issues raised by Dr. Stroll as of paramount
significance. If even a fraction of the claims
which Jesus made for himself, and which his
followers made for him, are true, then the
uncommitted will find themselves faced with
what Paul Tillich has well termed a "shaking
of the foundations," the necessity for a complete realignment of personal philosophy.

On the other hand, if Jesus' claims are un-
founded, then the Apostle Paul was absolutely correct when he wrote, "If Christ is not
risen from the dead, then we [Christians] are
of all men most miserable." Astute observers
of our neurotic epoch seem to be more concerned about the running out of the spiritual
rather than the natural fuel supply of the
world. And the question of the historical
validity of Jesus' claims bears directly upon
this 20th-century religious bankruptcy. In
spite of our radically different viewpoints on
the *de facto* validity of the historical portrait
of Jesus presented in the New Testament
documents, I believe that Dr. Stroll would
heartily second me when I express agreement
with the following statement by Millar
Burrows of Yale, the foremost American
expert on the Dead Sea scrolls:

"There is a type of Christian faith, ...
rather strongly represented today, [that] re-

*ds the affirmations of Christian faith as
onfessional statements which the individual
accepts as a member of the believing community, and which are not dependent on reason or evidence. Those who hold this position
will not admit that historical investigation can
have anything to say about the uniqueness of
Christ. They are often skeptical as to the
possibility of knowing anything about the
historical Jesus, and seem content to dispense
with such knowledge. I cannot share this
point of view. I am profoundly convinced
that the historic revelation of God in Jesus of
Nazareth must be the cornerstone of any faith
that is really Christian. Any historical question about the real Jesus who lived in Pales-
tine nineteen centuries ago is therefore funda-
mentally important.*"[2]

Four Errors

Granted the "fundamental importance" of
the question Professor Stroll raises, how correct is he in arguing concerning Jesus that
"the information we have about Him is a
composite of fact and legend which cannot
reliably be untangled"? Professor Stroll's
argument involves four major fallacies, and
these vitiate his entire presentation. Two of

---

[2]*More Light on the Dead Sea Scrolls* (New York:
Viking Press, 1958), p. 55.

these fallacies are of a historical character, and two are of a philosophical-logical nature. Taken together, they destroy his argument not only in historical and philosophical respects, but also in the theological sphere, since Christian theology cannot be divorced from logic and history. Let it be noted that I am not criticizing Dr. Stroll as a theologian (he himself expressly stated in his lecture that he was "not a theologian"). But I am claiming that he overstepped scholarly bounds in making his historical judgments and that he commits philosophical blunders incongruous with his academic specialization. What are Dr. Stroll's four errors? We shall mention them briefly now and come back to each in turn as our discussion proceeds.

Modern authorities: First, he relies almost exclusively upon the judgments of modern "authorities" in dealing with the question of the reliability of the New Testament documents.

The proper scholarly procedure is, of course, to face the documentary problems directly, by way of the accepted canons of historical and literary method. Professor Stroll himself points up this type of logical fallacy when he writes in his popular manual, *Philosophy Made Simple: "It is not the prestige of an authority which makes a statement true or false, but rather the citing of evidence either to confirm or disconfirm* [sic] *the statement.*"[3] Moreover, the modern "authorities" cited by Professor Stroll are consistently of a particular kind: They represent a radical tradition of New Testament criticism which reflects 19th-century rationalistic presuppositions (e.g., A. Schweitzer), and which issues in the Form-criticism school (*formgeschichtliche Methode*) of Dibelius and Bultmann, an approach regarded as misleading and outmoded by much of recent biblical scholarship. For example, and this instance is typical, A. H. McNeile of Trinity College, Dublin, and C. S. C. Williams of Merton College, Oxford, present seven thoroughly damning criticisms of the *Formgeschichte* approach.[4] We shall take up some of these criticisms later. What we wish to stress at this point is Professor Stroll's apparent lack of awareness of such criticisms.

Primary documents: Second, Dr. Stroll commits the unpardonable historical sin of neglecting primary documents. The earliest records of Christianity we possess are not the Gospel accounts but the letters of Paul. Dr. Stroll dispenses with these in one paragraph of nine lines in his twenty-page paper, on the

---

[3] Avrum Stroll and Richard H. Popkin, in the Doubleday "Made Simple Books" series (Garden City, N.Y.: Doubleday, 1956), p. 165; Stroll's italics.

[4] *Introduction to the Study of the New Testament,* 2nd ed. (Oxford: Clarendon Press, 1955).

remarkable grounds that "all of them have at one time or other been challenged as genuine" and that "Paul never met Jesus."

In fact, except for the so-called Pastoral Epistles and Ephesians, it would be next to impossible to find any competent present-day scholarship that denies the Pauline authorship of the corpus of letters purporting to have been written by him. That Paul had not himself been one of Jesus' original disciples is of minor significance when we remember that the author of one of the four Gospels (Luke) also wrote the Book of Acts, in which every effort is made to show that Paul's teachings about Jesus were accepted by the original apostles as fully consistent with their own remembrance of Jesus' message.

Begging the question: Third, Professor Stroll again violates his own philosophical canons by committing the logical error of *petitio principii:* "begging the question." In Stroll's *Philosophy Made Simple,* we again read: *"The Fallacy of Begging the Question ... occurs when either the same statement is used both as a premise and a conclusion in an argument, or when one of the premises could not be known to be true unless the conclusion were first assumed to be true."*[5] How does this circular argumentation

---

[5] Stroll and Popkin, p. 165.

operate in Professor Stroll's own discussion of Jesus' existence? He writes, "Even if there were reason to believe some of the material [in the Gospels] to express eye witness accounts of Jesus' life, the accretion of legend, the description of miracles performed by Jesus, which exist in these writings make it difficult, if not impossible, to extract from them any reliable historical testimony about the events described."

Here Dr. Stroll says that *regardless* of the question of eyewitness testimony, he rejects the authenticity of the Gospel accounts on the ground that they attribute miracles to Jesus. But how does one know whether miracles occurred in connection with Jesus' life unless he investigates the primary documents? Obviously Dr. Stroll is arguing in a circle and presupposing that miracles did not in fact occur in Jesus' life. As C. S. Lewis effectively points out in his work, *Miracles,* in the course of analyzing Hume's classic argument against miracles, *"Now of course we must agree with Hume that if there is absolutely 'uniform experience' against miracles, if in other words they have never happened, why then they never have. Unfortunately, we know the experience against them to be uniform only if we know that all the reports of them are false. And we can know all the reports to be false only if we know already that miracles have never occurred. In fact, we are arguing in a circle.*"[6] As we shall see in the second chapter, no historian can legitimately rule out documentary evidence simply on the ground that it records remarkable events; if the documents are sufficiently reliable, the remarkable events must be accepted even if they cannot be successfully explained by analogy with other events or by an *a priori* scheme of natural causation. L. J. McGinley's criticism of Bultmann, upon whom Dr. Stroll heavily relies, can as well be applied to him: "Whenever Bultmann denies the historic worth of a passage because of the supernatural content, he has ceased to be . . . an historian evaluating sources . . . and his criticisms have no value in the study of the Gospel text."

Essene messiahs: Last, Professor Stroll erroneously explains the "unhistorical" picture of Jesus in the New Testament documents as the product of a "messianic fever" characteristic of the Palestinian Jews living under the yoke of Roman oppression in the first century of our era. He parallels the Essene "messiahs" of the Dead Sea scrolls with Jesus and argues that the "psychological instability" of the time produced a divine Christ out of an eschatologically-orientated Nazarene teacher by the

---

[6]*Miracles* (New York: Macmillan, 1947), pp. 121-124.

21

name of Jesus.

As we shall show later, this entire argument demonstrates a baleful and inexcusable ignorance of the nature of Jewish messianic expectation at the time of Christ. Historically it can be proven beyond question that on every important point Jesus' conception of himself as Messiah differed radically from the conceptions held by all parties among the Jews. Particularly it cannot be harmonized with the Essene "Teacher of Righteousness" described in the scrolls from the Dead Sea. Moreover, as we shall also see, the transformation of a human Jesus to a divine Christ was a task of which neither the apostolic company nor Paul was psychologically or ethically capable, even if Jesus had met their stereotyped messianic expectations, which he did not. Here Professor Stroll has stepped onto quicksand where his unhistorical allegations are totally incapable of bearing philosophical weight.

2

THE NEW TESTAMENT DOCUMENTS

Is the New Testament valid historically? This question is central to those who are ready to consider Christ once they are sure the Gospels are accurate.

In the previous chapter we looked at four errors commonly made by those who answer with a No. Specifically the four errors we examined were made by Professor Avrum Stroll, formerly at University of British Columbia and now at University of California at San Diego.

This chapter moves to the positive side. Can we get a reliable picture of Jesus' claims from the New Testament?

We won't naively assume the "inspiration" or "infallibility" of the New Testament records and then by circular reasoning attempt to prove what we have previously assumed. We will regard the documents, even though today they are usually printed on fine India paper with verse numbers, only as documents, and we will treat them as we would any other historical materials. Our procedure will avoid Professor Stroll's first error (that of deferring to modern, rationalistic "authorities"). We shall go directly to the documents themselves and subject them to the tests of reliability employed in general historiography and literary criticism. These tests are well set out by C. Sanders, as bibliographical, internal, and external.[1] (Incidentally, since Sanders is a professor of military history, it seems unlikely that I will be criticized for theological bias.)

Bibliographical Test

This first test refers to the analysis of the textual tradition by which a document reaches us. In the case of the New Testament documents, the question is this: Not having the original copies, can we reconstruct them well enough to see what they say Jesus claimed? The answer to this question is an unqualified Yes. Sir Frederic G. Kenyon, formerly director and principal librarian of the British Museum, summarizes the textual advantage of the New Testament documents over all other ancient manuscripts by writing, *"In no other case is the interval of time between the composition of the book and the date of the ear-*

---

[1]*Introduction to Research in English Literary History* (New York: Macmillan, 1952), pp. 143 ff.

liest extant manuscripts so short as in that of the New Testament. The books of the New Testament were written in the latter part of the first century; the earliest extant manuscripts (trifling scraps excepted) are of the fourth century—say, from 250 to 300 years later. This may sound a considerable interval, but it is nothing to that which parts most of the great classical authors from their earliest manuscripts. We believe that we have in all essentials an accurate text of the seven extant plays of Sophocles; yet the earliest substantial manuscript upon which it is based was written more than 1400 years after the poet's death. Aeschylus, Aristophanes, and Thucydides are in the same state; while with Euripides the interval is increased to 1600 years. For Plato it may be put at 1300 years, for Demosthenes as low as 1200."[2] (For confirmation of these intervals between date of composition and date of earliest substantial text, together with numerous other examples, see F. W. Hall's list.[3])

---

[2]*Handbook to the Textual Criticism of the New Testament*, 2nd ed. (London: Macmillan, 1912), p. 5.

[3]"MS. Authorities for the Text of the Chief Classical Writers" by F. W. Hall in his *Companion to Classical Texts* (Oxford: Clarendon Press, 1913), pp. 199 ff.

But even this is not the whole story. Since the time when Kenyon wrote the above words, numerous papyri portions of the New Testament documents have been discovered. These go back to the end of the first century and bridge the 250 to 300 year gap of which Kenyon spoke. In evaluating these discoveries shortly before his death, Kenyon concluded, *"The interval, then, between the dates of original composition and the earliest extant evidence becomes so small as to be in fact negligible, and the last foundation for any doubt that the Scriptures have come down to us substantially as they were written has now been removed. Both the* authenticity *and the* general integrity *of the books of the New Testament may be regarded as finally established."*[4]

Moreover, as A. T. Robertson, the author of the most comprehensive grammar of New Testament Greek, wrote, "There are some 8,000 manuscripts of the Latin Vulgate and at least 1,000 for the other early versions. Add over 4,000 Greek manuscripts and we have 13,000 manuscript copies of portions of the New Testament. Besides all this, much of the

---

[4]*The Bible and Archaeology* (New York and London: Harper, 1940), pp. 288-89; Kenyon's italics.

New Testament can be reproduced from the quotations of the early Christian writers."[5] To be skeptical of the resultant text of the New Testament books is to allow all of classical antiquity to slip into obscurity, for no documents of the ancient period are as well attested bibliographically as the New Testament.

Internal Evidence

In this second test, historical and literary scholarship continues to follow Aristotle's dictum that the benefit of the doubt is to be given to the document itself, not arrogated by the critic to himself.[6] This means that one must listen to the claims of the document under analysis, and not assume fraud or error unless the author disqualifies himself by contradictions or known factual inaccuracies. In the case of the Pauline letters we must give considerable weight to their explicit claim to have been written by the Apostle. In the case of the whole gamut of New Testament documents we must take the authors seriously when they say, again and again, that they are

---

[5] A. T. Robertson, *Introduction to the Textual Criticism of the New Testament* (Nashville, Tenn.: Broadman Press, 1925), p. 70.

[6] Aristotle, *Art of Poetry (De Arte Poetica),* 1460b-1461b.

recording eyewitness testimony or testimony derived from equally reliable sources.

Examples can be multiplied. Here are a few. Luke's Gospel begins with the words, "Inasmuch as many have undertaken to compile a narrative of the things which have been accomplished among us, just as they were delivered to us by those who from the beginning were eyewitnesses and ministers of the word, it seemed good to me also, having followed all things closely for some time past, to write an orderly account for you, most excellent Theophilus, that you may know the truth concerning the things of which you have been informed."

The Fourth Gospel claims to have been written by an eyewitness to the crucifixion. In John 19:35 the author says, "He who saw it has borne witness—his testimony is true, and he knows that he tells the truth. . . ." I John, in its opening lines, likewise affirms eyewitness contact with Jesus: "That which was from the beginning, which we have heard, which we have seen with our eyes, which we have looked upon and touched with our hands, concerning the word of life—the life was made manifest, and we saw it, and testify to it, and proclaim to you the eternal life which was with the Father and was made manifest to us—that which we have seen and heard we proclaim also to you. . . ."

Sometimes the internal evidence of primary historical authority is not as direct as in the above instances, but is no less decisive. For example, C. H. Turner pointed out that Mark's Gospel reflects an eyewitness account of many scenes, for when the third person plural passes on to a third person singular involving Peter, we have the indirect equivalent of first person direct discourse, deriving from the Apostle.[7] Such internal considerations, both direct and indirect, provide a weighty basis for the claim that the New Testament documents are reliable historical sources.

External Evidence

In this test, the question is asked: Do other historical materials confirm or deny the internal testimony provided by the documents themselves? Careful comparison of the New Testament documents with inscriptions and other independent early evidence has in the modern period confirmed their primary claims. For example, Sir William M. Ramsay came to his conclusion after years of painstaking archeological and geographical investigation of Luke's Gospel. He rejected the negatively critical attitude to Luke taken by the

---

[7]*A New Commentary on Holy Scriptures,* Pt. iii, pp. 42-124.

19th-century Tübingen school. He wrote, "Luke's history is unsurpassed in respect of its truthworthiness."[8] Moreover, as to the authors and primary historical value of the Gospel accounts, confirmation comes from independent written sources. Papias, bishop of Hierapolis around A.D. 130, writes as follows on the basis of information obtained from the "Elder" (Apostle) John: *"The Elder used to say this also: Mark, having been the interpreter of Peter, wrote down accurately all that he [Peter] mentioned, whether sayings or doings of Christ; not, however, in order. For he was neither a hearer nor a companion of the Lord; but afterwards, as I said, he accompanied Peter, who adapted his teachings as necessity required, not as though he were making a compilation of the sayings of the Lord. So then Mark made no mistake, writing down in this way some things as he [Peter] mentioned them; for he paid attention to this one thing, not to omit anything that he had heard, nor to include any false statement among them."*[9]

Of the Gospel according to Matthew,

---

[8] *The Bearing of Recent Discovery on the Trustworthiness of the New Testament* (reprint ed.; Grand Rapids, Mich.: Baker, 1953), p. 81.

[9] I quote from Papias, as recorded in Eusebius' *Historia ecclesiastica*, III. 39.

Papias says, "Matthew recorded the oracles in the Hebrew [i.e., Aramaic] tongue,"[10] and the acceptance the book received in the primitive Church argues strongly for its early date and historical value. McNeile and Williams wrote, "[Matthew's] Gospel was the first favourite in the early Church although it lacked the prestige of the two chief centers of Christendom, Rome and Ephesus; and the prestige also of the two chief apostolic names, Peter and Paul. And the strongly Judaic elements in it would have discredited it if it had appeared in the second century. All of which imply its early, widely known, and apostolic credit."[11]   Another superlative external testimony to the primacy of the Gospel accounts is provided by Irenaeus, bishop of Lyons, who writes, *"Matthew published his Gospel among the Hebrews [i.e., Jews] in their own tongue, when Peter and Paul were preaching the gospel in Rome and founding the church there. After their departure [i.e., death, which strong tradition places at the time of the Neronian persecution in 64], Mark, the disciple and interpreter of Peter, himself handed down to us in writing the substance of Peter's preaching. Luke, the follower of Paul, set*

---

[10]*Ibid.*

[11]*Introduction to the Study of the New Testament,* 2nd ed. (Oxford: Clarendon Press, 1955), p. 33.

*down in a book the gospel preached by his
teacher. Then John, the disciple of the Lord,
who also leaned on his breast [this is a reference to John 13:25 and 21:20], himself produced his Gospel, while he was living at
Ephesus in Asia.''*[12]

The value of Irenaeus' remarks is especially
great because he had been a student of Polycarp, bishop of Smyrna, martyred in A.D. 156
after being a Christian for 86 years. Polycarp
in turn had been a disciple of the Apostle
John himself. Irenaeus had often heard from
Polycarp the eyewitness accounts of Jesus received from John and others who had been
personally acquainted with Jesus.[13]

We have now looked at powerful bibliographic, internal and external evidence. Competent historical scholarship must regard the
New Testament documents as coming from
the first century and as reflecting primary-
source testimony about the person and claims
of Jesus.

Specifically, present-day scholars date the
more important New Testament materials as
follows: the Pauline letters, A.D. 51-62;
Mark's Gospel, 64-70; the Gospels according
to Matthew and Luke, 80-85; Acts, shortly

---

[12] *Adversus haereses,* III. 1 (*ca.* 180).
[13] See Eusebius, *H.E.,* V. 20.

after Luke, which is really "Part One" of the two-part work; John's Gospel, no later than 100.

It should be emphasized that the dates here given are in general the latest possible ones for the books in question; there is excellent reason for earlier dating in most cases. For instance, Luke-Acts should probably be dated prior to 64, since Paul almost certainly died in persecution by Nero, yet Acts does not record his death. As a sensitive barometer to the current archeologically-based trend toward even earlier dating of these documents, we have the statement of the world's foremost biblical archeologist, W. F. Albright (whom, incidentally, Dr. Stroll cites at one point in his lecture, but not on this issue): "In my opinion, every book of the New Testament was written by a baptized Jew between the forties and the eighties of the first century A.D. (very probably sometime between about A.D. 50 and 75)."[14]

Form Criticism

In the last chapter I mentioned Professor Stroll's heavy reliance upon the work of a radical school of New Testament critics, the so-called *formgeschichtliche Methode* school of

---

[14]Quoted in an interview for *Christianity Today*, 18 Jan. 1963.

Dibelius and Bultmann. We are now in a position to see why this school has been steadily losing ground in scholarly circles during the last two decades. The form critics attempt by literary analysis to "get behind" the New Testament documents as they have come down to us. For example, the Gospels are assumed to be the end product of a process of oral tradition that was shaped and freely altered by the early Church according to its own needs—according to its *Sitz im Leben.*

Remarkably enough, this approach had already been flogged to death in the history of Homeric criticism, in an attempt to "get behind" the *Iliad* and the *Odyssey* as we have them. The result was complete chaos, for in the absence of any objective manuscript evidence to indicate where one "pre-literary" source left off and another began, the critics all differed with one another. H. J. Rose in discussing the dreary history of the problem, writes, "The chief weapon of the separatists has always been literary criticism, and of this it is not too much to say that such niggling word-baiting, such microscopic hunting of minute inconsistencies and flaws in logic, has hardly been seen, outside of the Homeric field, since Rymar and John Dennis died."[15]

---

[15] *Handbook of Greek Literature from Homer to the Age of Lucian* (London: Methuen, 1934), pp. 42-43.

In Dibelius, Bultmann and company, such flaw hunting has been seen in the New Testament field since Rose's day, but its weaknesses are now widely recognized. The method depends on rationalistic presuppositions against the supernatural, as we previously indicated, and leaves the gates wide open to subjective interpretation. It principally falls down because the time interval between the writing of the New Testament documents as we have them and the events of Jesus' life which they record is too brief to allow for communal redaction by the Church.

John Drinkwater, in his *English Poetry,* has rejected this approach in the study of English ballads, and, as McNeile and Williams correctly note, "No Gospel section passed through such a long period of oral tradition as did any genuine ballad."[16]

This is not to say that New Testament writers did not ever employ sources. We have seen that Luke expressly asserts that he did so. But with the small time interval between Jesus' life and the Gospel records, the Church did not create a "Christ of faith" out of a simple, moralistic Jesus. We know from the Mishna that it was Jewish custom to memorize a Rabbi's teaching, for a good pupil was like a "plastered cistern that loses not a

---

[16]McNeile and Williams, *Introduction,* p. 58.

drop."[17] And we can be sure that the early Church, impressed as it was by Jesus, governed itself by this ideal. Moreover, none of the form-critical researches has ever been successful in yielding a non-supernatural picture of Jesus, for "all parts of the Gospel record are shown by these various groupings to be pervaded by a consistent picture of Jesus as the Messiah, the Son of God."[18]

Conclusion

Here is a clear statement of the implications of the evidence that has been presented. F. F. Bruce, whom we have just quoted, is one of the foremost contemporary experts on the Dead Sea scrolls and presently serves as Rylands Professor of Biblical Criticism and Exegesis in the University of Manchester. He writes as follows of the primary-source value of the New Testament records: *"The earliest preachers of the gospel knew the value of . . . firsthand testimony, and appealed to it time and again. 'We are witnesses of these things,' was their constant and confident assertion. And it can have been by no means so easy as some writers seem to think to in-*

---

[17]*Mishna Aboth*, II. 8.

[18] F. F. Bruce, *The New Testament Documents: Are They Reliable?* 5th ed. (London: Inter-Varsity Fellowship, 1960), p. 33.

vent words and deeds of Jesus in those early years, when so many of His disciples were about, who could remember what had and had not happened. Indeed, the evidence is that the early Christians were careful to distinguish between sayings of Jesus and their own inferences or judgments. Paul, for example, when discussing the vexed questions of marriage and divorce in I Corinthians vii, is careful to make this distinction between his own advice on the subject and the Lord's decisive ruling: 'I, not the Lord,' and again, 'Not I, but the Lord.'

"And it was not only friendly eyewitnesses that the early preachers had to reckon with; there were others less well disposed who were also conversant with the main facts of the ministry and death of Jesus. The disciples could not afford to risk inaccuracies (not to speak of wilful manipulation of the facts), which would at once be exposed by those who would be only too glad to do so. On the contrary, one of the strong points in the original apostolic preaching is the confident appeal to the knowledge of the hearers; they not only said, 'We are witnesses of these things,' but also, 'As you yourselves also know' (Acts ii. 22). Had there been any tendency to depart from the facts in any material respect, the possible presence of hostile witnesses in the audience would have *served as a further corrective."*[19]

What, then, does a historian know about Jesus Christ? He knows, first and foremost, that the New Testament documents can be relied upon to give an accurate portrait of him. And he knows that this portrait cannot be rationalized away by wishful thinking, philosophical presuppositionalism or literary maneuvering. What exactly that portrait shows, and the radical consequences of it for each one of us, will be set out in the next chapter.

---

[19] *Ibid.*, pp. 45-46.

3

GOD CLOSES IN

What can we know for sure about the historic Jesus? In the last chapter we discovered that on the basis of the accepted canons of historical method—bibliographic, internal and external evidence—the New Testament documents must be regarded as reliable sources of information.

We learned that the documentary attestation for these records is so strong that a denial of their reliability carries with it total skepticism toward the history and literature of the classical world. We found the New Testament books to contain eyewitness testimony to the life and claims of Jesus, and to have been in circulation while friends and foes who had known Jesus were still alive and able to refute exaggerated, inaccurate or unwarranted statements about him.

Now, if you are not inclined in the direction of Christianity, as I was not when I entered university, the most irritating aspect of the line of argument I have taken is probably this: It depends in no sense on theology. It rests solely upon historical method, the kind of method all of us have to use in analyzing historical data, whether Christians, rationalists, agnostics or Tibetan monks. Perhaps at this point we can understand why C. S. Lewis, the great Renaissance English scholar, in describing his conversion from atheism to Christianity, writes, *"Early in 1926 the hardest boiled of all the atheists I ever knew sat in my room on the other side of the fire and remarked that the evidence for the historicity of the Gospels was really surprisingly good. 'Rum thing,' he went on. 'All that stuff of Frazer's about the Dying God. Rum thing. It almost looks as if it had really happened once.' To understand the shattering impact of it, you would need to know the man (who has certainly never since shown any interest in Christianity). If he, the cynic of cynics, the toughest of the toughs, were not—as I would still have put it—'safe,' where could I turn? Was there then no escape?"*[1]

Subsequently, says Lewis, "God closed in on me." How "God closes in" when we face the implications of historically reliable New Testament documents is the subject of this

---

[1] *Surprised by Joy* (New York: Harcourt, Brace, 1956), pp. 223-24.

chapter. We shall examine, in the primary documents that we validated in the last chapter, the picture of Jesus that appears there.

As we noted at the beginning of the first chapter, Jesus was especially concerned to bring his contemporaries to an accurate conception of himself. We may assume that he would want us also to arrive at a conception of him that is consistent with his real personality. No one wants to be misunderstood. And it is vital in the case of Jesus, who has had such an influence on world history, that misunderstanding be eliminated at all cost.

Yet in the twentieth century many have tended to create Jesus in the image of the time rather than to find out what the documents say about him. A bizarre, though typical, example is Bruce Barton's work, which attained great popularity a generation ago, titled, *The Man Nobody Knows: A Discovery of the Real Jesus.* The title was more fitting than Barton realized, for he clearly demonstrates that the Jesus of history is a man he doesn't know. Here are some representative chapter titles, referring to Jesus: "The Executive," "The Outdoor Man," "The Sociable Man," "The Founder of Modern Business." It is the last appellation that the author (himself, inevitably, a businessman) particularly stresses. Indeed, the book's title page quotation reads: "Wist ye not that I must be about my Father's business?"

But such dehistoricizings of Jesus are by no means limited to popular literature. Ironically, professional theologians have been more responsible than almost any other people in the twentieth century for producing unhistorical Jesuses. For example, we have the evaluation of Jesus given by Walter E. Bundy: "In our modern approach to Jesus we must leave him where and how and what he was, as real as he was—human. . . . In all of his life and work Jesus placed himself on the side of humanity. Speculation only separates him from us and makes him increasingly unreal. There are very definite religious dangers in deification—dangers destructive of Christianity."[2]

As a liberal modern of the twentieth century, Bundy's book paints a purely human portrait of Jesus and warns against the dangers of regarding him as divine. But what, in fact, was Jesus like? Is he pictured in the reliable documentary sources as Barton's "business executive," as Bundy's simple moral teacher (a Western Confucius going about giving people good advice that they didn't want anyway), or as someone far different from the ideals of twentieth century humanism?

---

[2] *The Religion of Jesus* (Indianapolis: Bobbs-Merrill, 1928), p. 324.

46

To answer this question we must strike behind the welter of modern "reconstructions"
of Jesus' life. We must go to the primary
sources themselves. Only then will we avoid
what C. S. Lewis in another work describes as
the demonic creation of imaginary Jesuses.
Screwtape, an elder devil, instructs his
nephew on the fine art of antidocumentary
temptation: *"In the last generation we pro-
moted the construction of . . . a 'historical
Jesus' on liberal and humanitarian lines; we
are now putting forward a new 'historical
Jesus' on Marxian, catastrophic, and revolu-
tionary lines. The advantage of these constructions, which we intend to change every
thirty years or so, are manifold. In the first
place they all tend to direct men's devotion to
something which does not exist, for each 'historical Jesus' is unhistorical. The documents
say what they say and cannot be added to;
each new 'historical Jesus' therefore has to be
got out of them by suppression at one point
and exaggeration at another, and by that sort
of guessing (brilliant is the adjective we teach
humans to apply to it) on which no one
would risk ten shillings in ordinary life, but
which is enough to produce a crop of new
Napoleons, new Shakespeares, and new
Swifts, in every publisher's autumn list."*[3]

[3] *The Screwtape Letters* (new ed.; London: Bles,
1961), pp. 103-104.

Warnings

In going to the documents to determine the *de facto* historical picture of Jesus, as distinct from Screwtapean constructions, we should keep two important caveats in mind. First, red-letter Bibles notwithstanding, no attempt will be made to distinguish Jesus' conception of himself from the New Testament writers' conceptions of him. All efforts to make such a distinction (and radical theological scholarship has frequently aimed at this kind of separation) are pointless and doomed to failure from the outset, because Jesus' words themselves have come to us by way of the New Testament writers.

However, the inability to distinguish Jesus' claims for himself from the New Testament writers' claims for him should cause no dismay, since (1) the situation exactly parallels that for all historical personages who have not themselves chosen to write (e.g., Alexander the Great, Augustus Caesar, Charlemagne). We would hardly claim that in these cases we can achieve no adequate historical portraits. Also, (2) the New Testament writers, as we saw in the previous chapter, record eyewitness testimony concerning Jesus and can therefore be trusted to convey an accurate historical picture of him.

A second preliminary caveat has to do with the approach we take to discovering Jesus' nature. We have no right to begin with the presupposition that Jesus can be no more than a man. For then, obviously, our conclusions may simply reflect our preconceptions instead of representing the actual content of the documents. We must, in other words, objectively try to discover the picture Jesus and his contemporaries had of him, whether we agree with it or not. The question for us is not whether Jesus is pictured as a man. Virtually no one today would question this, for the records tell us that he was hungry and tired, that he wept, that he suffered and died, in short, that he was human.

The question we face today is whether he was depicted as no more than a man.

It is instructive that the early church had to face the heresy of docetism, which did question Jesus' humanity. The docetists were so impressed by the evidence for Jesus' divinity that to them he only "seemed" (Greek: *dokein*) to be a man. But for us as humanistically-oriented moderns, the divinity of Jesus is the question, and only the documents can provide the answer to it.

What do the documents say? They say unequivocally and consistently that Jesus regarded himself as no less than God in the flesh, and that his disciples, under the pressure of his own words and deeds, came to regard him in this same way. Let us consider the prime New Testament records, in chronological order, and follow them by a significant passage from an early non-biblical source.

Paul

We begin with the letters of Paul, since they are the earliest materials we possess that bear on primitive Christianity. They date from between A.D. 51 and 62, and are firmly wedded to the Gospel records by way of Luke-Acts, where the stamp of approval is placed upon Paul by the original apostles. We can thus quote Paul without hesitation. Baur and the Tübingen school of the nineteenth century were unsuccessful in driving a wedge between Jesus and Paul, and present-day biblical scholarship has rejected their approach and conclusions.[4]

Paul affirms the divine character of Jesus in three unequivocal ways: First, he applies to Jesus the Greek word *kyrios,* "Lord," which was used in the pre-Christian Greek translation of the Old Testament (the Septuagint) as the equivalent of the most important Hebrew name of God, *Yahweh,* or *YHWH.* Note the implications of this. Paul, a monotheistic Jew, trained under the great Rabbi Gamaliel and therefore thoroughly conversant with the Old

---

[4]See J. G. Machen's classic, *The Origin of Paul's Religion* (Grand Rapids: Eerdmans, 1965).

Testament, ascribes to Jesus a word employed to render into Greek the most holy name of the one God. Consider as an example of Paul's identification of Jesus with the God of the Old Testament the following passages:

"Turn to me and be saved, all the ends of the earth! For I am God, and there is no other. By myself I have sworn, from my mouth has gone forth in righteousness a word that shall not return: 'To me every knee shall bow, every tongue shall swear.'" (Is. 45:22-23)

". . . At the name of Jesus every knee should bow, in heaven and on earth and under the earth, and every tongue confess that Jesus Christ is Lord, to the glory of God the Father." (Phil. 2:10-11)

Here Paul takes an Old Testament passage expressing in the most lofty and explicit terms the majesty and oneness of God, and applies it directly to Jesus, whom he refers to as *kyrios*. Instances of this kind can be multiplied with ease; see, for example, 2 Thessalonians 1:9 (quoting Isaiah 2:10, 19, 21); 1 Corinthians 1:31 and 2 Corinthians 10:17 (quoting Jeremiah 9:23 f.); 1 Corinthians 10:9 (quoting Numbers 21:5 f.), and compare the composite work, *Who Say Ye That I Am?*[5]

---

[5] W. C. Robinson, ed. (Grand Rapids, Mich.: Eerdmans, 1949), pp. 133ff.

Paul affirms the deity of Jesus in a second way. With the phrases "our God and Father himself, and our Lord Jesus" (1 Thess. 3:11) and "our Lord Jesus Christ himself, and God our Father" (2 Thess. 2:16), he uses a *singular* verb. This makes patently clear that for him, Jesus and the God of the Old Testament were conceived of as an essential unity. This conclusion is made even stronger (if it were possible) since both phrases appear in prayers. Thus Paul believed that prayer could be directed indiscriminately to God the Father or Jesus. Third, Paul held that Jesus would reappear as divine Judge at the end of the age: *". . . and to grant rest with us to you who are afflicted, when the Lord Jesus is revealed from heaven with his mighty angels in flaming fire, inflicting vengeance upon those who do not know God and upon those who do not obey the gospel of our Lord Jesus. They shall suffer the punishment of eternal destruction and exclusion from the presence of the Lord and from the glory of his might, when he comes on that day to be glorified in his saints, and to be marveled at in all who have believed, because our testimony to you was believed." (2 Thess. 1:7-10)*

Mark

Next we must look at the earliest of the four Gospels, Mark, which was written no later than A.D. 64-70 by a companion of the apostle Peter. At the outset of this book Mark makes clear that Jesus should be personally identified with the God of the Old Testament. He writes, "The beginning of the gospel of Jesus Christ, the Son of God. As it is written in Isaiah the prophet, 'Behold, I send my messenger before thy face, who shall prepare the way; the voice of one crying in the wilderness: Prepare the way of the Lord, make his paths straight' " (Mk. 1:1-3).

Here Mark has quoted Malachi 3:1, but with a highly significant alteration. The prophetic verse reads: "Behold, I [YHWH] will send my messenger, and he shall prepare *the way before me.*" But Mark changes the verse so that it reads "he shall prepare *thy way,*" that is, Jesus' way. Mark is saying that when the God of the prophets spoke of preparing for his own coming, he was speaking of the preparation for Jesus' coming. Or, putting it as simply as possible, Jesus is the God of the prophets. This affirmation, which in the Greek text of Mark stands like a red flare at the beginning of the book, is confirmed again and again throughout the book. In Mark 2, Jesus forgives sin, and the scribes correctly recognize that he is blaspheming if he is not God, for only God can forgive sins. "My son, your sins are forgiven," Jesus says, and the scribes respond, "Why does this man speak thus? It is blasphemy!" (Mk. 2:5-7)

But elsewhere is Jesus not perhaps regarding himself simply as a man with special privileges? Does he not use the expression "Son of man"? This expression, which humanists have often appealed to as equivalent to "representative humanity" is really one of the loftiest ascriptions given to God's Messiah in the Old Testament (see Daniel 7:13). Jesus expressly applies this imagery to himself at his trial, and brings upon himself condemnation for blasphemy.

"Again the high priest asked him, 'Are you the Christ, the Son of the Blessed?' And Jesus said, 'I am; and you will see the Son of man sitting at the right hand of Power, and coming with the clouds of heaven.' And the high priest tore his mantle, and said, 'Why do we still need witnesses? You have heard his blasphemy. What is your decision?' And they all condemned him as deserving death." (Mk. 14:61-64)

Although not much good can be said about the high priest at this kangaroo court, one thing is certain: He correctly recognized that Jesus was claiming to be no less than God incarnate, and that if he was not what he claimed, then he was a blasphemer.

Matthew
The Gospels according to Matthew /the apos-

tle) and Luke (a physician who accompanied Paul on his missionary journeys) were written no later than A.D. 80-85. Albright would say probably before 75. They present the same divine-human picture of Jesus given in Mark. The virgin birth account in these two Gospels is unequivocal. Even though the Hebrew word *almah* in the Isaiah prophecy can mean "young woman" as well as "virgin," the Greek *parthenos* employed in Matthew and Luke must mean "virgin." As Karl Barth has correctly noted, the virgin birth demonstrates that God the Father uniquely entered history in Jesus and was the active agent in his advent.

Moreover, the Jesus of these Gospels makes absolute claims for himself that are unthinkable apart from deity. For example, Jesus says, "So every one who acknowledges me before men, I also will acknowledge before my Father who is in heaven; but whoever denies me before men, I also will deny before my Father who is in heaven. . . . He who finds his life will lose it, and he who loses his life for my sake will find it" (Mt. 10:32-33, 39).

Jesus states his divine life-purpose as follows: ". . . The Son of man came not to be served but to serve, and to give his life as a ransom for many" (Mt. 20:28). This assertion is also integral to Mark's Gospel (Mk. 10:45). Jesus' last words in Matthew are also consonant only with deity, for they ascribe to him the divine attributes of omnipotence and omnipresence and place him on the same plane as the Father: *"And Jesus came and said to them, 'All authority in heaven and on earth has been given to me. Go therefore and make disciples of all nations, baptizing them in the name of the Father and of the Son and of the Holy Spirit, teaching them to observe all that I have commanded you; and lo, I am with you always, to the close of the age.' "* (Mt. 28:19-20)

Acts
In the Book of Acts, written by Luke, Paul is converted to Christianity in the recognition, on the Damascus road, that Jesus is *kyrios* (Acts 9:5). The entire apostolic preaching, as C. H. Dodd has so effectively pointed out, centers on the Lordship of Jesus. "What must I do to be saved?" is the question. "Believe on the Lord Jesus and you shall be saved," is the consistent answer (cf. Acts 16:30-31). In fact, "there is salvation in no one else for there is no other name under heaven given among men, by which we must be saved" (Acts 4:12).

John
The fourth Gospel is thoroughly Christocentric and identifies the Eternal Father with

the historic Jesus at every point. The prologue affirms Jesus' pre-existence and eternal oneness with God. The "I am" sayings ("I am the light, bread," etc.) allude to the "I am that I am" revelations of the God of the Old Testament (see Exodus 3:14). Salvation occurs only through Jesus; he says in John 14:6, "I am the way, and the truth, and the life; no one comes to the Father, but by me." And the numerous miracle-signs performed by Jesus in this Gospel, culminating in the great sign, the resurrection, are recorded "that you may believe that Jesus is the Christ, the Son of God, and that believing you may have life in his name" (Jn. 20:31).

The Gospel reaches its climax with the "doubting Thomas" incident, in which Thomas is confronted by the resurrected Jesus and confesses, "My Lord and my God" (Jn. 20:28). This picture of Jesus in John's Gospel is especially meaningful when we remember that the apostolic authorship of the book is attested by Irenaeus, who knew Polycarp, a disciple of John himself.

Conclusion
Thus a consistent portrait of Jesus emerges from the earliest New Testament documents: a divine portrait of one who could say, "He who has seen me has seen the Father" (Jn. 14:9). And this is how Christians from the

earliest days have regarded him. In the first description of Christian worship from the pen of a non-Christian we read: "On an appointed day they [Christians] were accustomed to meet before daybreak, and to recite a hymn antiphonally to Christ, as to God." This significant passage comes from a letter written c. 112 by the governor of Bithynia, Pliny the Younger, to the Emperor Trajan (Epis. X, xcvi). From that day to this all Christians, Eastern Orthodox, Roman Catholic and Protestant, have worshipped Christ as God, on the basis of the historically impeccable testimony of Jesus' own followers and of those who knew them intimately.

The Jesus of the primary documents, then, is one hundred and eighty degrees removed from the "businessman" of Barton, the humanistic moralist of Bundy, the catastrophic reformer of the Marxists, and from all other twentieth-century attempts to create him in the image of cultural idealism.

We may not like the Jesus of the historical documents; but like him or not, we meet him there as a divine being on whom our personal destiny depends.

4

A HISTORIAN'S APPEAL

Suppose that the New Testament documents portray a divine Christ. Was he in fact divine?

Logically, if Jesus was not divine, as the records unequivocally claim he was, we are reduced to three, and only three, interpretations of the New Testament data:

(1) Jesus claimed to be the Son of God but knew he was not. He was a charlatan.

(2) Jesus thought he was the Son of God, but actually he was not. He was a lunatic.

(3) Jesus never actually claimed to be the Son of God, though his disciples put this claim in his mouth. So, the disciples were charlatans, lunatics, or naive exaggerators.

I believe that a careful consideration of these three interpretations will show that no one of them is consonant with history, psychology or reason, and that therefore, by process of elimination, we are brought to affirm Jesus' deity not only as a claim, but also as a fact.

Charlatan?

The idea of Jesus as a charlatan—as an intentional deceiver who claimed to be something he knew he was not—has never had much appeal, even among fanatical anti-religionists. Jesus' high ethical teachings and noble personal character have made such an interpretation extremely improbable. W. E. H. Lecky, the great nineteenth-century historian and certainly no believer in revealed religion, wrote of Jesus, "The character of Jesus has not only been the highest pattern of virtue, but the strongest incentive to its practice, and has exerted so deep an influence, that it may be truly said, that the simple record of three short years of active life has done more to regenerate and to soften mankind, than all the disquisitions of philosophers and than all the exhortations of moralists."[1]

This judgment has been echoed thousands of times through the centuries by men of all or no religious persuasions. Is it possible that such a Jesus would have committed one of the most basic moral errors of all, allowing the end to justify the means, and based his entire life and ethical teachings upon a colossal lie as to his real nature? He was at pains to

---

[1] *History of European Morals from Augustus to Charlemagne,* 2nd ed. (London: Longmans, Green, 1869), II, 88.

convince the men of his time that the devil is a liar and the father of lies, and that those who lie are the devil's children (Jn. 8:44). Would he himself then have lied concerning the essence of his own character and purpose? To answer anything but an unqualified No is to renounce sound ethical judgment.

Lunatic?

But perhaps Jesus' claims to deity and messiahship had their source not in intentional deception, but in Jesus' honest misunderstanding of his nature. This is the position taken by Schweitzer in 1906 in his *Quest of the Historical Jesus,* a work which was epochal because of its recognition of the eschatological character of Jesus' message, but which is almost universally regarded by New Testament scholars today as setting out a "historical Jesus" who reflects Schweitzer's own rationalistic presuppositions.

Schweitzer felt it necessary to vindicate his Jesus (who misunderstood his own nature) from the charge of psychiatric illness. Schweitzer's *Psychiatric Study of Jesus* (his Strassburg M.D. dissertation of 1913) is a Herculean but ineffective attempt to show that Schweitzer's purely human Jesus could be sane and yet think of himself as the eschatological Son of man who would come again at the end of the age, with the heavenly host, to judge the world. In actuality, as Dr. Winfred Overholser, past president of the American Psychiatric Association, has noted in his foreword to the latest English edition of Schweitzer's thesis, Schweitzer has not ruled out paranoia in the case of a purely human Jesus: "Some paranoids manifest ideas of grandeur almost entirely, and we find patients whose grandeur is very largely of a religious nature, such as their belief that they are directly instructed by God to convert the world or perform miracles."[2]

We cannot avoid the conclusion that Jesus was deranged if he thought of himself as God incarnate and yet was not. Noyes and Kolb, in the latest (5th) edition of their standard medical text, *Modern Clinical Psychiatry,* characterize the schizophrenic as one whose behavior becomes autistic rather than realistic—as one who allows himself to "retreat from the world of reality."[3] What greater retreat from reality is there than a belief in one's divinity, if one is not in fact God? I know that you would immediately summon the men in white coats if I seriously made the claims for myself that Jesus did. Yet, in view

[2] *The Psychiatric Study of Jesus* (Boston: Beacon Press, 1958), p. 15.
[3] *Modern Clinical Psychiatry* (Philadelphia and London: Saunders, 1958), p. 401.

of the eminent soundness of Jesus' teachings, few have been able to give credence to the idea of mental aberration. Indeed, the psychiatrist J. T. Fisher has asserted recently what many others have been implicitly convinced of:

"If you were to take the sum total of all authoritative articles ever written by the most qualified of psychologists and psychiatrists on the subject of mental hygiene—if you were to combine them and refine them and cleave out the excess verbiage—if you were to take the whole of the meat and none of the parsley, and if you were to have these unadulterated bits of pure scientific knowledge concisely expressed by the most capable of living poets, you would have an awkward and incomplete summation of the Sermon on the Mount. And it would suffer immeasurably through comparison. For nearly two thousand years the Christian world has been holding in its hands the complete answer to its restless and fruitless yearnings. Here . . . rests the blueprint for successful human life with optimum mental health and contentment."[4]

But one cannot very well have it both ways: If Jesus' teachings provide "the blueprint for successful human life with optimum

---

[4]J. T. Fisher and L. S. Hawley, *A Few Buttons Missing* (Philadelphia: J. B. Lippincott, 1951), p. 273.

mental health," then the teacher cannot be a lunatic who totally misunderstands the nature of his own personality. Note the absolute dichotomy: If the documentary records of Jesus' life are accurate, and Jesus was not a charlatan, then he was either God incarnate as he claimed or a psychotic. If we cannot take the latter alternative (and, considering its consequences, who really can follow this path to its logical conclusion?), we must arrive at a Jesus who claimed to be God incarnate simply because *He was God.*

False Portrait?

But, is there not a third way of escaping the horns of this dilemma? Could not Jesus' followers have painted a false portrait of him, out of an intentional or unintentional desire to put him in the best possible light? It is held that a "messianic fever" pervaded the Jews under first-century Roman domination, and led some of them to deify Jesus of Nazareth.

This interpretation, though perhaps superficially plausible, has no more to commend it than the interpretations we have just considered. It falls down on three decisive counts. First, all types of Jewish messianic speculation at the time were at variance with the messianic picture Jesus painted of himself, so he was a singularly poor candidate for deification. Second, the apostles and evangelists were psychologically, ethically and religiously incapable of performing such a deification. Third, the historical evidence for Christ's resurrection, the great attesting event for his claims to deity, could not have been manufactured. Let's take up each of these in turn.

In order for the Jews of Jesus' time to have messianized him, it would have been necessary for Jesus' teachings and conception of himself to accord with the main outlines of the messianic hope held by his contemporaries. However, in all essential points this was not the case. Consider, for example, Jesus' attitude toward the Gentiles. Edersheim, late Grinfield Lecturer on the Septuagint at Oxford, writes,

"In view of all this [first-century Jewish antipathy toward the heathen in Palestine], what an almost incredible truth must it have seemed, when the Lord Jesus Christ proclaimed it among Israel as the object of His coming and kingdom, not to make of the Gentiles Jews, but of both alike children of one Heavenly Father; not to rivet upon the heathen the yoke of the law, but to deliver from it Jew and Gentile, or rather to fulfil its demands for all! The most unexpected and unprepared-for revelation, from the Jewish point of view, was that of the breaking down of the middle wall of partition between Jew and Gentile, the taking away of the enmity of

*the law, and the nailing it to His cross. There
was nothing analogous to it; not a hint of it to
be found, either in the teaching or the spirit
of the times. Quite the opposite. Assuredly,
the most unlike thing to Christ were His
times.*"[5]

The great Jewish scholar S. W. Baron pre-
sents a detailed discussion of "Messianic Expectations" at the time of Jesus. He writes
that "Zealot activists expected the redeemer
to appear sword in hand and to lead the people against Rome's military power," and that
"most apocalyptic visionaries, on the other
hand, expected redemption in the shape of a
cosmic cataclysm, out of which would emerge
a new world with the chosen people marching
toward final salvation at the head of a transformed mankind."[6] He also says that even
those with "less high-flown expectations"
were convinced that messiah would bring
back "the remnants of the lost Ten Tribes"
and reunite Israel and Judah.

Does this sound like the Jesus of the documents, who said, "My kingdom is not of this
world"? Baron regards Jesus "as an essentially

---

[5] *Sketches of Jewish Social Life in the Days of
Christ* (reprint ed.; Grand Rapids, Mich.: Eerdmans, 1957), pp. 28-29.

[6] *Social and Religious History of the Jews,* 2nd ed.
(New York: Columbia University Press, 1952), II,
58 ff.

Pharisaic Jew,"[7] but the primary records present the Pharisees as his chief opponents, for he continually set himself above the law and refused to be bound by the legalistic traditions of the Pharisees.

As for the party of the Sadducees, no one would argue that common ground existed between Jesus and them, for they were rationalistically inclined. (They denied the general resurrection of the body, the existence of angels, etc.) And though mutual hate and mistrust colored the relations between Pharisees and Sadducees, both parties were so disturbed by Jesus that they united against him (Mt. 16:1, etc.). The single fact that official Jewry crucified Jesus for blasphemy is sufficient ground for rejecting the idea that Jesus fulfilled the messianic dreams of the time.

But what about the Essene sect of the Dead Sea scrolls, to which Professor Stroll makes reference? Millar Burrows[8] and F. F. Bruce,[9] among other experts on the scrolls, have shown beyond question that the Essene conception of a "Teacher of Righteousness" differed in all essential points from Jesus' messianic views. Burrows demonstrates that

---

[7] *Ibid.,* p. 67.

[8] *More Light on the Dead Sea Scrolls* (New York: Viking Press, 1958), pp. 65-73.

[9] *Second Thoughts on the Dead Sea Scrolls* (London: Paternoster Press, 1956), *passim.*

"there is no hint of a pre-existent Messiah in the Qumran texts"; that "nowhere is there a suggestion of anything miraculous in the birth of the teacher of righteousness"; that "the saving efficacy of the death of Christ has no parallel in the beliefs of the covenanters concerning either the teacher of righteousness or the coming Messiah" (indeed, that "the idea of a suffering Messiah . . . was known at all in Judaism at that time is a debatable question").

Moreover, since the teacher of righteousness was not believed to rise from the dead until the general resurrection at the end of the age, whereas Jesus was believed to have risen directly following his crucifixion, "what for the community of Qumran was at most a hope was for the Christians an accomplished fact, the guarantee of all their hopes." Burrows goes on to show that "the term which Jesus most commonly used in referring to himself (Son of man) is one that does not occur at all in the Qumran literature as a Messianic designation," and, what is perhaps most significant of all, "there is no indication that the teacher of righteousness was considered divine in any sense."

To argue, then, that Jesus was deified or messianized because he fulfilled Essene messianic expectation is impossible on historical ground.

Note the point at which we have arrived: If anyone deified Jesus, it must have been his own disciples, against the entire pressure of first-century Jewish ideology. But, as Burrows correctly states: "Jesus was so unlike what all Jews expected the son of David to be that His own disciples found it almost impossible to connect the idea of the Messiah with Him."[10]

And even when they did become convinced that he was God's anointed, could they have deified him without cause? R. T. Herford, in discussing "The Influence of Judaism upon Jews from Hillel to Mendelssohn," says, "The Jewish religion throughout the whole of the period is based upon two main principles, the assertion of the undivided unity of God and the paramount duty of obedience to His declared Will."[11] Would then the disciples and followers of Jesus, steeped in the Jewish faith, have deified a mere man, thereby contradicting the central tenet of the Jewish faith, that "thou shalt have no other gods before me"?

Moreover, were these early followers of Jesus psychologically or temperamentally capable of carrying out such a deification process? Certainly they, no less than Jesus

---

[10] Burrows, p. 68.

[11] *Legacy of Israel* (Oxford: Clarendon Press, 1928), p. 103.

himself, were then charlatans or psychotics. Yet the picture of them in the documents is one of practical, ordinary people, down-to-earth fishermen, hardheaded tax gatherers, etc., and people with perhaps more than the usual dose of skepticism. Think of Peter returning to his old way of life after Jesus' death; think of "doubting" Thomas. Hardly the kind of men to be swept off their feet into mass hallucination of technicolor proportions.

What did finally and irrevocably convince the followers of Jesus that he was the one he claimed to be, God incarnate? What transformed them from a shocked and broken group after the crucifixion to a company that preached Jesus' message of salvation up and down the Roman world until the empire itself, and with it the Western world, became Christian? The answer lies in the resurrection, and a brief discussion of it will conclude our presentation.

Resurrection
Jesus was crucified in Jerusalem during the high festival of the Jewish religious year, the Passover. The city was teeming with people, and because of the involvement of mobs in the quasi-legal proceedings, it is clear that the public was well aware of what was transpiring. Since Jesus had claimed that he would rise

again after three days, and indeed had pointed to this event as the final proof of his claims to deity (Mt. 12:38-40; Jn. 2:18-22), the Jewish religious leaders made certain that guards were stationed at the tomb to prevent the disciples from stealing Jesus' body and maintaining that he had actually risen. However, according to the documents, Jesus did rise, bodily, and was seen again and again over a forty-day period, until he publicly ascended into heaven. The appearances are recorded with clinical detail:

"As they [the disciples] were talking, . . . there he was, standing among them. Startled and terrified, they thought they were seeing a ghost. But he said, 'Why are you so perturbed? Why do questionings arise in your minds? Look at my hands and feet. It is I myself. Touch me and see; no ghost has flesh and bones as you can see that I have.' They were still unconvinced, still wondering, for it seemed too good to be true. So he asked them, 'Have you anything here to eat?' They offered him a piece of fish they had cooked, which he took and ate before their eyes." (Lk. 24:36-43, NEB)

"The other disciples told him [Thomas], 'We have seen the Lord.' But he said to them, 'Unless I see in his hands the print of the nails, and place my finger in the mark of the nails, and place my hand in his side, I will not

believe.' *Eight days later, his disciples were again in the house, and Thomas was with them. The doors were shut, but Jesus came and stood among them, and said, 'Peace be with you.' Then he said to Thomas, 'Put your finger here, and see my hands; and put out your hand, and place it in my side; do not be faithless, but believing.' Thomas answered him, 'My Lord and my God!' "* (Jn. 20:25-28)

The records leave no doubt that the writers were well aware of the distinction between myth and fact, and that they were proclaiming the resurrection as factual. "We," they write, "did not follow cleverly devised myths when we made known to you the power and coming of our Lord Jesus Christ, but we were eyewitnesses of his majesty" (2 Peter 1:16). The factual character of the resurrection provided the disciples with the final proof of the truth of Jesus' claim to deity, and it provides the historian with the only adequate explanation for the conquering power of Christianity after the death of its founder. False messiahs of the time fell into obscurity because they could not back up their claims.

For example, Theudas in A. D. 44 promised a crowd that he would divide the waters of the Jordan river, and in A. D. 52-54 an unnamed "Egyptian" messiah gathered a crowd of 30,000 Jews and said that at his command the walls of Jerusalem would fall

down.[12] But both incidents ended in igno-
minious failure, accompanied by bloodshed at
the hands of the Roman soldiery. Christianity, however, flourished as a result of Jesus'
attested claim to conquer the power of death.

But can the modern man accept a "miracle" such as the resurrection? The answer is a
surprising one: The resurrection has to be
accepted by us just because we are modern
men, men living in the Einstein relativistic
age. For us, unlike people of the Newtonian
epoch, the universe is no longer a tight, safe,
predictable playing-field in which we know all
the rules. Since Einstein no modern has had
the right to rule out the possibility of events
because of prior knowledge of "natural law."

The only way we can know whether an
event can occur is to see whether in fact it has
occurred. The problem of "miracles," then,
must be solved in the realm of historical investigation, not in the realm of philosophical
speculation. And note that a historian, in
facing an alleged "miracle," is really facing
nothing new. All historical events are unique,
and the test of their factual character can be
only the accepted documentary approach that
we have followed here. No historian has a
right to a closed system of natural causation,

---

[12] Josephus, *Jewish War*, II, 13, 4.259; *Antiquities*,
XX, 8, 6.170.

for, as the Cornell logician Max Black has shown in a recent essay, the very concept of cause is "a peculiar, unsystematic, and erratic notion," and therefore "any attempt to state a 'universal law of causation' must prove futile."[13]

As Ethelbert Stauffer, the Erlangen historian, puts it, "What do we do [as historians] when we experience surprises which run counter to all our expectations, perhaps all our convictions and even our period's whole understanding of truth? We say as one great historian used to say in such instances: 'It is surely possible.' And why not? For the critical historian nothing is impossible."[14]

If the resurrection did occur, and the evidence for it is tremendous, then we cannot rule it out because we are unable to "explain" it by an *a priori* causal schema. Rather, we must go to the one who rose to find the explanation, and his explanation, though we may not like it, is that only God himself, the Lord of life, could conquer the powers of death.

Of course, attempts have been made to "explain" the resurrection accounts naturalistically. The German rationalist Venturini

---

[13] *Models and Metaphors* (Ithaca, N. Y.: Cornell University Press, 1962), p. 169.

[14] *Jesus and His Story* (New York: Knopf, 1960), p. 17.

suggested that Jesus only fainted on the cross and subsequently revived in the cool tomb. This "swoon theory" is typical of all such arguments: They are infinitely more improbable than the resurrection itself, and they fly squarely in the face of the documentary evidence. Jesus surely died on the cross, for Roman crucifixion teams knew their business (they had enough practice). He could not possibly have rolled the heavy boulder from the door of the tomb after the crucifixion experience.

And even if we discounted these impossibilities, what happened to him later? If we agree that he died and was interred, then the explanation that the body was stolen is no more helpful. For who would have taken it? Surely not the Romans or the Jewish parties, for they wished at all costs to squelch the Christian sect. And certainly not the Christians, for to do so and then fabricate detailed accounts of Jesus' resurrection would have been to fly in the face of the ethic their master preached and for which they ultimately died. As J. V. Langmead Casserley pointed out in his 1951 Maurice Lectures at King's College, London, the attempts to explain away the resurrection demonstrate that "the assertion of the resurrection is like a knife pointed at the throat of the irreligious man, and an irreligious man whose irreligion is reatened will fight for his own creation, his most precious possession, like a tigress fighting for her cubs."[15]

Note that when the disciples of Jesus proclaimed the resurrection, they did so as eyewitnesses and they did so while people were still alive who had had contact with the events they spoke of. In A. D. 56, Paul wrote that over 500 people had seen the risen Jesus and that most of them were still alive (1 Cor. 15:1 ff). It passes the bounds of credibility that the early Christians could have manufactured such a tale and then preached it among those who might easily have refuted it simply by producing the body of Jesus.[16]

The conclusion? Jesus did rise, and thereby validated his claim to divinity. He was neither charlatan nor lunatic, and his followers were not fablemongers; they were witnesses to the incarnation of God, and Jesus was the God to whom they witnessed.

A Historian's Appeal
Today, especially in university circles, agnosticism has become immensely fashionable. The days of the hidebound atheist appear to be

---

[15] *The Retreat from Christianity in the Modern World* (London: Longmans, Green, 1952), p. 82.
[16] Frank Morison, *Who Moved the Stone?* (new ed.; London: Faber & Faber, 1944), *passim*.

past, but his agnostic replacement is in many ways even farther from the intellectual mainline. The atheist at least has recognized the necessity of taking a position on ultimate matters. The agnostic, however, frequently makes a demi-god out of indecision. Actually, as Heidegger, Sartre and other contemporary existentialists stress, all life is decision, and no man can sit on the fence. To do so is really to make a decision, a decision against decision.

Historians, and indeed all of us, must make decisions constantly, and the only adequate guide is probability (since absolute certainty lies only in the realms of pure logic and mathematics, where, by definition, one encounters no matters of fact at all).

I have tried to show that the weight of historical probability lies on the side of the validity of Jesus' claim to be God incarnate, the Savior of man, and the coming Judge of the world. If probability does in fact support these claims (and can we really deny it, having studied the evidence?), then we must act in behalf of them. When Jesus said that he would spue the lukewarm out of his mouth, he was saying that action on his claims is mandatory. "He who is not with me is against me," he plainly taught.

And how do we act in behalf of his claims? In just one way. We come to the point of acknowledging that the ultimate problems of our existence, such as death and the self-centeredness that gives death its sting, can only be solved in his presence. We look away from ourselves to his death and resurrection for the answers to our deepest needs. We put ourselves into his hands.

What is the result of such a personal commitment to the risen Christ? I can myself attest to it: Freedom, for the servant of Christ is slave to no man. In a fearfully changing world, he is solidly grounded in an unchanging Christ, and therefore is free to develop his capacities to the fullest, under God.

If God is "closing in on you," why not let the gap be closed entirely? As Pascal so well put it, you have nothing to lose and everything to gain.

APPENDIX:
FAITH, HISTORY & THE RESURRECTION

On the occasion of Carl F. H. Henry's lecture series early in 1965 at Trinity Evangelical Divinity School in Deerfield, Illinois, several Chicago-area theologians shared in a vigorous panel discussion on problems of faith and history. Participants were Dr. William Hordern, then professor of systematic theology at Garrett Biblical Institute, Evanston; Dr. Jules L. Moreau, professor of church history at Seabury-Western Theological Seminary, Evanston; and Father Sergius Wroblewski, professor of New Testament and church history at Christ the King Seminary (Franciscan), West Chicago. Joining them were Dean Kenneth Kantzer and Professor Montgomery of Trinity, and Dr. Henry. This is the edited transcription of the discussion as it originally appeared in Christianity Today, *March 26, 1965.*[1]

[1] © 1965 by *Christianity Today*; reprinted by permission.

Dean Kantzer: The focus of our interest is on the nature of history, and the relationship which Jesus Christ bears to history in our Christian faith. Perhaps Dr. Henry will state the issues briefly for us, and then we will be asking one another some questions.

Dr. Henry: Frontier issues in the dialogue on the Continent at the moment include the relationship of revelation and history and the relationship of revelation and truth. At this breakpoint over faith and history the cleavage occurs between Barthian dialectical theology and Bultmannian existential theology, and then also between many post-Bultmannians and Bultmann himself, and finally also between the *Heilsgeschichte* scholars and the post-Bultmannians. The further question is raised over the connection between revelation and truth, which is a subject of debate among the dialectical theologians and which recalls Barth's modifications of his own point of view, and the consequent assault on Barth's views by both evangelical scholars and the Pannenberg school.

Dean Kantzer: If I remember correctly, you hold that the lack of objectivity in Barth's view of the relationship between Jesus and history represented a fatal weakness in the Barthian position, which led to a more easy victory of Bultmann in his distinction between the Christ of faith and the Jesus of history. Would you care to say just a further word about that?

Dr. Henry: Confessedly Barth's introduction of objectifying elements into his theology places a wide distance between Barth and the existential theologians, whether Bultmannian or post-Bultmannian. Yet the objectifying elements Barth introduced into his system are not really objects of historical research. And for all the objectifying factors with which he buttressed his doctrine of the knowledge of God, he agreed in spirit with Bultmann that God is not an object of rational knowledge. Both scholars reject the objectivity of God as an object of rational knowledge. Barth and Bultmann shared the fundamental dialectical premise that divine revelation is never objectively given—neither in historical events nor in concepts or words—and in agreement with this underlying premise Bultmann dispensed entirely with the objectifying elements that Barth sought to preserve with a surer instinct for biblical theology.

Dean Kantzer: Now, Dr. Hordern, we would be interested to know whether you agree that this was a flaw in Barth that made Bultmann's victory more easily accomplished.

Prof. Hordern: It seems to me that there is a great deal more objectivity in Barth than you imply. His revolt from existentialism was not quite so belated; he made it when he started writing his *Church Dogmatics*. He tore up the original version because it had too much existentialism in it. I am aware of the fact that Bonhoeffer spoke of Barth's revelational positivism, and I think that is a more apt criticism in some ways than to say that Barth does not have sufficient objectivity. He very definitely believed—quite apart from man's knowledge of it—that God was in Christ, that the Bible *is* (as he puts it in *Church Dogmatics* I/2) *the* Word of God, and that this is true whether or not man recognizes it. The real problem, when you raise the question of objectivity of history, is, What does one mean by *history?* And maybe also, What does one mean by *objectivity?*

If by history you simply mean investigation of what has happened in the past, it is very obvious that Barth's whole system was built upon the historical nature of the revelation, that it was an event that happened—that Jesus Christ was born of a virgin and raised from the dead. These are events that happened. But if by history you mean what so many people mean today, that which can be verified by modern historical method (and when that in turn means that by definition any miracle cannot have been historical), then it seems to me that Barth is forced to say that historical criticism cannot help the Christian faith, or that it cannot produce anything other than a non-biblical Jesus. *By definition* it cannot, if this is what one means by historical method, and this is what is widely meant. That is why Barth, speaking of the resurrection, can say, Of course this is not historical if by history (I am not quoting him verbatim) you have the concept that miracles are not historical by definition. But, he says (and I can imagine the twinkle in his eye), that doesn't mean it didn't happen. In other words, Barth is arguing that more has happened objectively— whatever we mean by that—than what would be discovered by historical method. But it seems to me there is more objectivity here in Barth than you have given reason to suppose.

Prof. Montgomery: I wonder what you would say—what Barth would say—if I claimed that in my backyard there is a large green elephant eating a raspberry ice cream cone, but that there is no way by empirical investigation to determine that he is there. Nonetheless, I maintain, as a matter of fact, that it is there in every objective and factual sense. Now I have a feeling that you would either regard this as a claim that the elephant is there and is subject to empirical investigation, or contend that it isn't there by the very fact that there is no way of determining the fact. I wonder if this doesn't point up the problem. To claim objectivity, but to remove any possibility of determining it, is by definition to destroy objectivity.

Prof. Moreau: Would you be willing to use, instead of this green elephant monstrosity, the body of the late Herbert Hoover out in Iowa?

Prof. Montgomery: The reason that I use my example is that I don't want an illustration which has merely natural repercussions. The problem here points to the question of the miraculous, and therefore I would like something bizarre in order to keep the aspect of miracle in view.

Prof. Hordern: I'm not sure that the miraculous is bizarre. But to carry out the analogy Barth would have to say that one who knows (before he goes to your garden and looks) that there is no such thing as a green elephant —if he then "sees" it, he will obviously say, I have hallucinations. No evidence is going to prove the reality of a green elephant to this man. When you have a concept of history which has decided before it investigates any empirical facts that dead men stay dead, then if this is what you mean by history (as many people do), historical investigation proves nothing.

Prof. Montgomery: Isn't this the very point: whether historical method necessitates the presupposition that the miraculous, whatever we mean by this, cannot take place? It seems to me that the confusion here is between historical method and what might be called historicism or historical prejudice. Historical investigation very definitely can take place on the empirical level without the positivistic presupposition that the nexus of natural causes cannot be broken. It seems to me that the question here is whether historical method, apart from that rationalistic presupposition, will or will not yield revelatory data concerning Jesus Christ. And if one says that it won't, then one strips away the meaning of the word "objectivity."

Prof. Hordern: But this, I think, is Barth's point; he does not use this precise formulation, but what you call historical method without historicism, Barth definitely approves.

Prof. Montgomery: Well, I get the impression that he would prefer not to speak of historical method at all in connection with the resurrection. He is willing to use it in connection with the death of Christ—with those events that are of a natural and normal type. But it appears to me that with regard to the resurrection, for example, there is a hesitancy that doesn't arise simply from Barth's refusal to take a rationalistic position on miracles. He seems unhappy with any use of historical method in relation to the resurrection.

Prof. Moreau: What kind of historical method would you use in connection with the resurrection, when in the first place I'm not sure you know what you mean by the word "resurrection"—or at least *I* don't know what you mean by the word "resurrection." You have submitted a whole set of active verb sentences.

Prof. Montgomery: The claim that somebody, as a matter of fact, rose from the dead following his death.

Prof. Moreau: That I don't think is what the Bible says. The Bible says somebody "was raised," and I'm not altogether sure that *ek nekron*—"from dead"—can be taken to mean "raised from the dead" in that sense.

Prof. Montgomery: Well, that's the sphere of death. I won't belabor the genitive.

Prof. Moreau: Well, I will, because I think it is pretty important. I don't think there is any word "resurrection" as such. I don't think the Bible talks conceptually.

Prof. Montgomery: Well, then, in concrete terms, take the question of a man rising from the dead. . . .

Prof. Moreau: What kind of historical method would you use to investigate that?

Prof. Montgomery: One has to determine empirically first of all whether this concrete man died, and secondly, whether after this event this concrete man engaged in normal human intercourse with other persons in a spatial-temporal situation.

Prof. Moreau: You think that historical method is capable of doing this?

Prof. Montgomery: Very definitely; but it's hardly capable of arriving at an *explanation,* of determining *how* it happened.

Prof. Moreau: Now that historical method has done this, *what good* is that kind of information?

Prof. Montgomery: Plenty, if you have a death problem—because you are obviously going to wonder why in thunderation this happened.

Father Wroblewski: I would hold that you can accept the apostolic testimony as historical, and I think that in doing that you follow historical method. When I read historians who tell me that Napoleon carried on a war, I am unable to see it, but I go by the testimony of those who did so, and of those who have sifted the evidence. And so I feel that I can accept the testimony of the apostles for the same reason. They saw, they didn't merely imagine; and to me that is historical testimony. I will admit to a subjective element, however. The apostles who reacted to the human Christ (or rather to the suffering servant), and then to the risen Christ, appraised him differently. Each Gospel has a different method because each gospel author took a certain *view* of Christ. That was in a way subjective because it was peculiar to *him*. But

91

even that was not achieved apart from the influence of the Holy Spirit.

Dean Kantzer: I wonder if I could sharpen the issue by referring to the green elephant again. There is no question (so far as our discussion here is concerned) as to its facticity. There really was a green elephant there—unless perhaps it was Saturday night! The question, is, *How one can know that the green elephant was there?* And now, carrying this analogy over to the resurrection the question is, How we can discern this facticity which we are admitting? Then comes the question, Is this a matter of history? Some are saying it is, and some are saying it isn't. On the surface it might look as though it were simply a matter of definition, of the definition of history: whether history is a study in which you rule out the supernatural. But as we proceeded it became perfectly obvious that this wasn't the whole point, that the issue goes beyond whether or not you define history one way or another. The issue is whether in theory the idea of presupposition-less history is possible. Or whether one believes that history is a methodology which one must engage in with the presupposition that miracles do not happen. With that kind of presupposition one couldn't under any circumstances find any historical data about the kind of event that we call resurrection. There

are those who, in other words, do not wish to
make the distinction that Dr. Hordern was
making (between a history that excludes
supernatural events and a history that
doesn't), and who prefer to say of Christ's
resurrection, "*Incredible*—this is the kind of
thing that nothing we have any right to call
history (with any sort of presupposition)
could touch!" Dr. Moreau, how do you feel
about this latter position?

Prof. Moreau: In part I think this is right.
In one sense history is knowledge of the past.
I think Father Wroblewski's statement about
a Napoleonic war is very interesting. But
that's perfectly accessible; you don't have to
depend on someone's testimony for that—not
really.

Father Wroblewski: But you are surely dependent on the testimony of reliable witness,
aren't you? You never saw Napoleon.

Prof. Moreau: But then you have the problem of the differences in Scripture.

Father Wroblewski: I think those differences in part at least are demonstrated by the
fact that the Scriptures are written from a
particular viewpoint. I don't think that the
question is defining what is the object of history. I think that the difficulty lies in what
you define as observable. If you decide from a
philosophical point of view that miracles are
impossible, necessarily as a historian you limit

vhat you can observe. I think that this is the difficulty between the right and the left, in the interpretation of Scripture. Bultmann, for instance, would deny, from a philosophical point of view, that there is any miracle, and therefore he would exclude a witness's power to observe anything miraculous—I mean a man rising from the dead, or anything like that.

Dean Kantzer: Do you think that the author of the Gospel of Luke thought that by inquiring from witnesses and by investigating sources you could come to the certainty of the events that are recorded in the Gospel of Luke?

Prof. Moreau: I'm not sure, and I'm not sure that's relevant. In the light of other knowledge about the past it would be interesting.

Father Wroblewski: Do you have more confidence in Napoleon's historians than in the gospel witnesses? Do you regard the fathers of the Church as "primitives" in science and in history?

Prof. Hordern: One of the best things that I read on the current historical problem is something that *Christianity Today* published not very long ago, which turned out to have been the inaugural address made by J. Gresham Machen in 1915. This shows you how theology goes around in circles. What is now the hottest issue was being discussed in a very interesting fashion there. I think Karl Barth would agree with that article, which is why I wonder about the debate over objectivity. But let's leave Karl Barth out of this; he is not here to defend himself. First of all, you have to recognize that there is a historical problem. For example, did Lee Oswald, unaided, without conspiracy, assassinate Kennedy? If this is a typical group of Americans, you divide 50-50 yes and no. Do you believe the Warren Commission's report? For the Gallup Poll, 50 percent of us do and 50 percent don't. It is a historical event that was investigated thoroughly, completely; probably no event in all history had such a thorough investigation of the facts so quickly.

Prof. Montgomery: Are you suggesting a statistical test of a historical truth?

Prof. Hordern: No, not at all! You could never hope to have an event investigated more thoroughly, more completely, than this assassination was investigated under the Warren Report. Yet it is not just "crackpots" that remain unpersuaded. It is not a matter of statistics. You cannot get absolute historical proof. And those who doubt the Warren Commission report say, Well, look; who did the investigating? Just one side there! Oswald didn't do the investigating; the American government did! What you've got here is what the American government wanted to find! And you can take the same attitude toward him who is talking about the resurrection of Jesus—the Christian. Always when you have a problem of history you have this kind of dubiousness.

Dr. Henry: Are you saying that, in principle, the question of the death of Napoleon is no different from the question of the death and resurrection of Christ—that both come under the same difficulties insofar as historical accessibility and research are concerned?

Prof. Hordern: In principle, yes. This is the problem of history in general. It's one thing to empirically investigate this green elephant today, if we can rush outside and he is there now. It is another thing to decide whether we have historical evidence to persuade us that he was there last Saturday. Now we must ask if the witnesses are reliable. Perhaps Saturday night is the night they go out on the town.

Dr. Henry: But suppose one argues that it was really there, yet insists that facticity cannot be determined by historical research—that in point of fact this was a confrontation that took place on "the rim" of history?

Prof. Hordern: You're going to make me defend Barth again; he's very capable of defending himself. But I would answer the question for myself. (Whether Barth would want me to say this or not, I'm not sure; perhaps it depends on where you draw your evidence from Barth. The historical question, What does Barth really think? is also a problem.) What does Machen do—when he argues for the historicity of the resurrection? He points to those facts that cannot really be disputed because all you have to do is open your New Testament and there they are. Here's a man writing who says, *I saw the risen Jesus!* There a community was formed, and here we have it today—and we have something pretty empirical here. Here something comes through two thousand years, and here it is. And then Machen argues: Which is more likely: that these disciples got together when Jesus died and said, "Isn't this horrible; let's pretend he rose from the dead," and started a movement, and endured persecution for a lie—or that he arose? And now if this is what you mean by the historical argument, fine. The Gospel does depend upon historical argument. If this does not make any kind of sense, then we would be pretty silly to believe it. On the other hand, it will never persuade any of my skeptical friends who know that dead men stay dead.

Prof. Montgomery: How do they know that?

Dr. Henry: They have a private pipeline to ultimate reality.

Prof. Montgomery: Isn't it at that very

point that the attack needs to be delivered—if I may succumb to military terminology. Isn't the area of difficulty not really the question of historicity but the question of presupposition with regard to the nature of the world? And it certainly can be shown that whoever enters an investigation with a presupposition such as Dr. Hordern describes feels that he has a kind of stranglehold on the universe—a stranglehold that simply can't be justified.

Prof. Hordern: Don't argue with me. I don't hold that position.

Prof. Montgomery: Granted: your presentation a moment ago was magnificent.

Prof. Hordern: Machen's presentation, actually. There is still a further point, though, if we come back to the death problem. Machen makes the other point, that on the basis of historical evidence we may not be persuaded but that ultimately we believe because in the context of the Church we meet the risen Christ. And, therefore, what makes reasonably logical the historical account of the past is ultimately something at which you might shrug your shoulders and say, Well, isn't that interesting?

Prof. Moreau: Too bad they didn't have a Society for Psychical Research there. They would have really gotten some good material. When we meet the risen Christ in our lives, then all this becomes significant and important to us.

Prof. Montgomery: But make a distinction on the question of appropriation: Appropriating the fact is not what makes it factual. This is the crucial consideration I think we tend to overlook; when, for example, Professor Hordern writes in his *Case for a New Reformation Theology* that religious objectivity can be arrived at only when we have faith in objectivity, he enters on a path that leads straight to solipsism. Apart from the distinction between the object (Christ historically resurrected, in the ordinary sense of "history"—*Historie*) and the subject (ourselves as believers in it) a clear distinction must be made.

Prof. Moreau: Maybe God can make such a distinction—I can't!

Father Wroblewski: What difference would it make whether he rose or not? I would like to know, what difference, if you cannot establish that Christ rose from the dead? Paul said that we who are in Christ are united with the risen Christ. If he didn't rise from the dead, we are miserable. In fact, Paul said we then are of all men *most miserable.* But apparently Dr. Moreau wouldn't be very miserable. What would bother you about all this?

Prof. Moreau: Come back to what the doctrine of the Holy Spirit is. What really makes the difference is whether or not there is some experience of the risen Christ at this moment in communal fellowship with him.

Father Wroblewski: And this makes what difference for what?

Prof. Moreau: Significance or non-significance.

Prof. Montgomery: But then I think I would have to ask the question, if I were a non-Christian, Why should I involve myself in this kind of a community rather than in, let's say, another community? What criteria are men to employ in order to justify a choice or decision?

Prof. Moreau: I simply refuse to become involved in dichotomies of that sort.

Father Wroblewski: I would see no reality to the experience of the risen Christ if I had no proof of his resurrection.

[*At this point Dean Kantzer welcomed questions from the floor.*]

Student: If Christ did not rise from the dead, how could I have any subjective benefits from the resurrection of Christ in my life today?

Prof. Moreau: There are two points I would make in reference to that. First, I did not say he was not raised from the dead. What I am really concerned about is whether or not there is any historical verification. As far as I'm concerned the empty tomb story is a purely figurative account, an expanding of something which is quite real in the sense of an experience. And I think it is inaccessible for historical inquiry. I did not say that God did not raise him from the dead. I insist on keeping that physical language.

Prof. Montgomery: But you would distinguish this from a "real" objectivity of the resurrection?

Prof. Moreau: I don't like that language.

Prof. Montgomery: But you distinguish between the resurrection and the empty tomb?

Prof. Moreau: I distinguish the statement that God raised Jesus from the dead from the statement that the empty tomb has anything to do with this in terms of inquiry or investigation or proof.

Dr. Henry: By what criteria do you distinguish this presence of the risen Christ from a mere immortality of influence?

Prof. Montgomery: And how do you know (this is a terribly irreverent question) that your experience of Christ in the heart differs from heartburn?

Prof. Moreau: I suppose ultimately I don't.

Student: I would like to ask Dr. Hordern a question in view of his use of the example of the shooting of President Kennedy supposedly by Oswald. I hesitate to accept this analogy completely because, as far as I know, there is no record that Oswald claimed that he was going to do this. If the record of the New

Testament writers is valid, I think there is a distinction here between the Christ event and the event of the shooting of John F. Kennedy, because of the claim here apparently that Christ was going to do his work. Maybe this accounts for the problem of so many people not believing the Warren Commission.

Prof. Hordern: To me the parallel between the Kennedy assassination and the crucifixion and resurrection of Jesus is simply the parallel that both are history to us. And the very fact that a history so close to us, so thoroughly investigated, still cannot beat down all possible doubts indicates to me that when we have some history two thousand years old, with much less material, and without the intensive investigation—without the FBI to help out— how much less certainty we can have on this basis.

I've been trying to locate myself with Dr. Moreau here; we obviously have a number of things in common. I would warn him, however, as Barth has warned Bultmann, that if you too easily get rid of that empty tomb you're probably falling into Docetism. But to me the thing that you cannot argue has been raised here a couple of times: If Jesus Christ did not rise from the dead, how can it all be important to me? You have two questions here. One, Did Jesus Christ rise from the dead?—which you can settle somewhere,

102

though I'm not quite sure where. And the other question is, What does it mean to me? Certainly my point is that before you even ask the question, Did Jesus Christ rise from the dead? you ask it only because it concerns you in some way. One man is concerned because he wants all dead men to stay dead and therefore he wants as an answer: No, he didn't rise. Another man wants to answer it another way. My point is simply that we have to make the historical judgment on the basis of our own experience. It seems to me I've got Machen on my side here, because he says that if we didn't actually know the living Christ now, we could not believe the history of the past. And I'm arguing that you don't independently solve the one question, Did he rise from the dead? and then ask, How do I appropriate this? or, What does it mean to me? but that these two are continually involved together. That doesn't mean, however, that you haven't any reason for this. You have a lot of reasons. There is a great difference between the guy who just shuts his eyes and believes and the fellow who doesn't—I know that Dr. Moreau has a lot of reasons for what he believes. But ultimately, if you really want to put it that way, none of us knows that we are even here, and a good philosopher could prove we aren't. We walk through this world as sojourners by faith and not by sight.

Student: The question, though, is, By faith in what? Ultimately we've got to get back to the question of what the ground of faith is. Otherwise someone can come along and, maintaining that we walk by faith and not by sight, take a position exactly contrary to yours or mine, and there won't be anything that the Christian proclamation can say in relation to this at all.

Student: I could push it back a little farther. You mentioned the rhythm of history, and that the character of the event was in question. It seems to me that one thing that distinguishes the data in connection with President Kennedy's assassination and the resurrection is the kind of material we have. Paul says this thing was not done in a corner. In the assassination we have an event which took place under the tightest security, deliberately obscured by the person who did it, and this is why the evidence is obscure. But in the case of Jesus, it was quite the opposite; it was right out in the open. I'd like to ask Dr. Henry if he believes that there is a distinction between the Napoleonic or Kennedy-assassination type of history and the Jesus-event, and if the real question isn't about the supernatural rather than simply a question of events.

Dr. Henry: When you ask a historical question, you can answer only in terms of historical research and historical method. The collective consciousness of the early Church, or my present psychological encounters of whatever nature, cannot give a decisive answer to the question of the historicity of an event some nineteen centuries ago. So I would agree with Professor Hordern that as history the New Testament saving events are subject to the same research as other historical events. There is, however, a broader frontier. Jesus Christ stepped into history from the outside; ultimately we do not explain him *in toto* from within history, but we explain history by him. And it is certainly true that there is more to the case for the resurrection of Jesus Christ than historical fact. The Christian does not argue the case for the risen Christ only in terms of the historical data. There is the relevance of Pentecost; I certainly would not want to drop the Book of Acts and the Epistles out of the case for the risen Christ. But when it comes to the question of a historical resurrection from the dead and the matter of the empty tomb, this can be answered only in terms of historical research and testimony. And I quite grant that one cannot get to absolute certainty in terms of historical method; absolute certainty is always something communicated by the Spirit of God. But the very heart of the apostolic preaching falls out if you lose the historical ingredient.

Prof. Montgomery: Let me set up another analogy than Dr. Hordern's appeal to the Kennedy assassination. It is fairer to compare the resurrection to other events of classical times, because it's in the same general time area and therefore the amount of data is perhaps more comparable. I majored in classics in college, and to my amazement I never heard any questioning of the events of the classical period as to their *per se* historicity despite the fact that these are based on much less data than the resurrection of Christ. For example, the existence of Plato depends upon manuscript evidence dated over a thousand years later. If we must begin with sheer faith in order to arrive at the event-character of the resurrection, then we are going to drop out not simply the resurrection but a tremendous portion of world history, which I don't think we're prepared to do.

Prof. Hordern: I couldn't care less whether Caesar crossed the Rubicon or not. It doesn't make any difference to me. I'm not going to lead my life any differently tomorrow either way; nothing stands or falls with it. Perhaps if I made my living out of history, and was battling with some other colleague, we might have ourselves a real battle among historians over precisely such questions. There is hardly anything that has happened in past history that doesn't get debated by historians at some

106

time or other. Most of us couldn't care less, however; we have no real involvement with this. But here we have a story that comes to us from two thousand years ago, and if it is true, then my destiny not only here but hereafter depends upon this story—and you ask me to believe it on the basis only of the generally unreliable historical data?

Prof. Montgomery: No, not quite. I say only that the historical probabilities are comparable to those of other events of classical times. Therefore there is an excellent objective ground to which to tie the religion that Jesus sets forth. Final validation of this can only come experientially. But it is desperately important not to put ourselves in such a position that the event-nature of the resurrection depends wholly upon "the faith." It's the other way around. The faith has its starting point in the event, the objective event, and only by the appropriation of this objective event do we discover the final validity of it. The appropriation is the subjective element, and this must not enter into the investigation of the event. If it does, the Christian faith is reduced to irrelevant circularity.

Father Wroblewski: Dr. Hordern, as you realize, there is resistance today to the acceptance of miracles as proof. Why is it that Scripture itself urges miracles, the empty tomb, the charismatic gifts, the coming down of the Holy Spirit as proof? Would you resist those proofs, if the Scripture itself urges such proofs?

Prof. Hordern: Show me where the Scripture urges these as proofs.

Dr. Henry: What of Paul's emphasis that Jesus was seen by more than 500 persons at once in proof of the resurrection?

Prof. Montgomery: The Christian faith is built upon Gospel that is "good news," and there is no news, good or bad, of something that didn't happen. I personally am much disturbed by certain contemporary movements in theology which seem to imply that we can have the faith regardless of whether anything happened or not. I believe absolutely that the whole Christian faith is premised upon the fact that at a certain point of time under Pontius Pilate a certain man died and was buried and three days later rose from the dead. If in some way you could demonstrate to me that Jesus never lived, died, or rose again, then I would have to say I have no right to my faith.

Prof. Moreau: I couldn't do that, because you are beginning with the assumption that it did take place.

Father Wroblewski: I hold that the apostolic witness to the miraculous in the life of Christ is equivalent to the kind of evidence history is based on. The apostles saw and heard these things happen in time and space, and I have no reason to disbelieve the soundness of their testimony. Rather I have more reason to trust their powers of observation because they signed their testimony in blood. Scholars who deny the miraculous do so on philosophical grounds in the face of Scripture's insistence on the miraculous as evidence. It is true that the evidence is not absolute if only because the "appointed witnesses" were few and their written record puzzling. But this is peculiar about biblical evidence: It leaves the intellect somewhat hesitant that the act of faith may arise more from the Holy Spirit's operation than intellectual proof.

Prof. Moreau: The current preoccupation with the facticity of the circumstances surrounding the event called the resurrection reflects a concern for historical verification which is quite foreign to the attitude of the early church. The "proof" that God had raised Jesus from among the dead was the experience of the living Lord in the community. The narrative of the empty tomb and the embroidery around it served an apologetic purpose rather than a verificational one. The involved argument advanced by St. Paul (1 Cor. 15:35-58) seems only to underline this contention.

Prof. Hordern: The life of Jesus is a historical event like other historical events and is known through the reports of those who witnessed it. It differs from other historical events because we have a unique opportunity to test the reliability of the witnesses. They tell us that Jesus did not stay dead and that we can know him as the risen Lord. As a result, our evaluation of the gospel records cannot be separated from our relationship to the risen Christ today.